Death Sucks,

Life Doesn't Have To

Brea Behn

ISBN: 978-1-61296-473-7

PUBLISHED BY BLACK ROSE WRITING

www.blackrosewriting.com

Printed in the United States of America

Suggested retail price $13.95

Death Sucks, Life Doesn't Have To is printed in Cambria

ACKNOWLEDGMENTS

There are so many people in my life that have gotten me where I am today. First, my parents for having me and my twin despite the risks and battles to get us here, raising us to the best of your abilities and the magnitude of support and love since. Second, to my husband who has been my rock many times and who has supported me in this crazy wonderful author journey. Finally, to my family, friends and fans who support and encourage me in my literary efforts, accept me for who I am and no matter where they are in my life hold a dear place in my heart. Thank you all.

Death Sucks,

Life Doesn't Have To

INTRODUCTION

Death is something that is all around us and happens to us all. However, it is also something we do not talk about often. Death found me when I was just fifteen years old. Death took the person in my life that was closest to me.

On May 19, 1999, my twin brother, Brad William Crouse, died from an accident with a handgun.

Now, before I continue, you need to know a few things about me to understand who I am. I was born a twin. My twin and I were raised in rural Wisconsin. I have two older brothers (six and nine years older). My parents divorced when I was nine. I have moved thirteen times in my life. I went to school at a private Christian elementary school. Like a lot of kids in a private religious school, I didn't like it all that much and my stay did not end well. I switched to public school in seventh grade. At the same time my mom started dating again. I hated it. I got in with the wrong crowd and got into the worst things in my entire life. I smoked. I drank. I stole. I lied. I got Ds and Fs in school. I became suicidal. I was thirteen. Then my twin brother gave me some great but simple advice. Find new friends. So I did. I became happy again. I found my place in school. I got decent grades. My mom remarried and I got a new brother and two sisters—one who is my age and became my best friend. Life was looking up.

Then my twin died. That is where I will begin my story.

CHAPTER ONE

MY STORY

There is no question—death is not easy. Even when we think we are ready. Even when it finds us when we least expect it. It hurts!

Death found me when I least expected it. I was fifteen. I was happy. May 18, 1999 started like any other day. I got up early and tickled my twin brother awake to get ready for school. His girlfriend *Ana came in and ruined my work by getting into bed with him and going back to sleep. We went to school and were looking forward to the weekend and the summer ahead.

At home after school, my stepsister Lisa and I had our friend Erika over to jump on the trampoline. Brad meanwhile was mowing the lawn and then went in to play Nintendo. We jumped for a long time and then we went inside and while I got ready for bed, my stepsister and Erika went to Brad's room to watch him do something on the computer. I went to talk with my mom in her room and we heard a car pull in. Brad's friend Derek from the "wrong crowd" came in the house with one of his friends. Both my mom and I were surprised because Brad had been on the outs with Derek since Brad had been spending most of his time with his girlfriend. They went upstairs and joined my friends and Brad in his room.

It was getting late and I was tired, so my mom and I were going to go upstairs to tell everyone it was time to go home. We got to the bottom of the stairs and heard a very loud bang. I remember stopping, my heart pounding, and listening very hard for laughter at dropping something or a verbalized swear word at shooting a hole in the wall. But then someone screamed and my mom and I ran up the stairs.

After that God gave me the gift of shock, and the rest of the night is in bits and pieces in my memory, like a movie that is on fast-forward and delay all at once. I remember running into my twin brother's room and seeing red—red on the floor, red on the walls and red on my brother. I remember my brother being the only one in the room. He was sitting in his swivel chair in front of the computer desk with his head slumped. If I didn't know any better I would have thought he had dozed off in his chair and was going to wake up laughing. Looking back on it now, it feels like that moment stretched on for a long time. I remember seeing his girlfriend's ring on his pinky; I remember he was wearing one of his classic Brad black t-shirts, I remember mentally stripping all the red out of the room as if it weren't really there.

No one stayed to help Brad or us. The four other people in the room had run out while we ran in. It was I who helped my mom get Brad out of the chair and lay him on the floor. I remember she yelled at me to get a pillow. I helped her put it under his head and saw my twin brother's brains on his face and a hole in his temple. My mom tells me she did CPR on him and I helped, but I don't remember that.

I remember lying on the floor next to him sobbing, with my face inches from his, and through my tears I saw one single tear flow down his cheek. That more than anything will burn in my memory forever. At that moment I knew I would never speak to my twin brother again and that was his way of saying goodbye. Twin's have bonds far deeper than can be logically explained. I felt my brother leaving then. I felt his confusion, his regret, and his fear.

Someone, I don't remember who, made me go downstairs and I collapsed at the bottom of the stairs and just sobbed. I only moved when the paramedics made me so they could get up the stairs. I remember how they looked down at me and I saw the looks on their faces. They knew it was bad. They brought him by me on the stretcher and I was screaming and sobbing. He was all strapped down and they were moving very fast.

The next thing I remember is lying on my mom's bed downstairs sobbing and screaming. It must have been for hours because a police officer came in and told my oldest brother they were going to have to "give me something" if I didn't stop. For some reason his words scared me enough to make me stop crying. I remember thinking he had no right to turn off my grief.

After that I remember my oldest brother getting a phone call. He came in and told me Brad was brain dead. I was so consumed with grief I thought that meant he was gone forever, and I would never see him again, but I was wrong. In my shock, I faded out.

Later, I was in someone's car on the way to the hospital where Brad was. My two brothers were with me as well. We got to the hospital and I became confused because they were telling us we couldn't see him yet because he was in ICU. In my fog I thought, "How can he be in the ICU if he is dead?"

Hours later I got to see Brad. I found out that although my twin brother was shot in the head his heart still wouldn't stop. He was young, healthy, and as stubborn as I am, so his heart kept beating until they got to the hospital. He was in a bed with every tube imaginable hooked up to him. His right eye was covered with a bandage and his whole head was covered in gauze. His face looked awful. His head was very swollen. His eye that was showing was swollen too. I tried not to look at his face. Instead I held onto his arm, the only place visible without tubes, and tried to cry, but with my shock I had run out of tears.

For the next horrible day I did nothing but sleep, cry, and be sick. Everyone tried to get me to eat, but food seemed like something so ridiculous. I watched the people I love come one by one by one to cry, hug me, and see Brad for the last time with his heart beating. Yet, I still could not cry.

The hardest thing I had to do that day was call my best friend Jamie, from our Christian school, to tell her what had happened to Brad. She was our friend from the time we met in preschool and it was the hardest thing I have ever had to tell anyone. I remember my mom wanted me to tell her myself and she handed me the phone. My hand was shaking so hard I could barely hold it. I don't remember exactly what I told her, but years later she told me that I said, "Brad's been shot in the head. He is dead." She reacted exactly how I felt: she screamed. She bravely went to her school that day to tell the rest of our Christian school friends the horrible news.

The next day they told us what we already knew. Brad was brain dead. The exploding-tip bullet had completely shredded the top half of his brain, leaving him a shell with a young athletic heart that wouldn't quit on its own.

They asked if we would like to donate his organs. My mom and dad sat me down and told me I knew Brad better than anyone and asked me what he would want. I told them he was the kindest person I had ever known and that he would be proud to help others who could use the organs he no longer could use. I asked if I could be alone with him. I sat down next to him and practically yelled: "If I made the wrong decision you don't have to do it, Brad; just let your body die; make your heart stop if you don't want to!" But the monitor kept blipping away and I knew Brad had made his final decision the way he made them all, with love and kindness for everyone but himself. For the first time in days I burst into tears once more. My whole family waited for the doctor to come get us and tell us Brad's heart had truly stopped beating and he was free of the shell his body had become.

After they were done with their modern-day miracle, they let us see his body. They had taken every organ and tissue that would change someone's life or save it and finally they stopped his beautiful heart to save a life too.

My mom asked me if I wanted to see him after and I numbly said yes. My brothers, dad, my mom and I came into the room and his whole body except his shoulders was covered with a sheet. The doctor had explained to us not to move the sheet because of how he looked after they harvested his organs. I was in first and I remember staring at him thinking it couldn't be real. I placed my hand on his shoulder without thinking and the cold I felt was not a normal cold. It was a cold that went against the life I had always felt there before. It was a cold that was the opposite of life. What I felt was death. There are no words that can describe that kind of cold. In my memory I was the only one in my family who touched him.

My memory fast-forwards to when we went to the funeral home to plan his funeral. My parents took me along to help make the decisions because once again I knew Brad the best. Ironically, my brother and I had talked about death in our late-night talks. I knew he wanted to be cremated because the thought of "worms eating me" disgusted him. I also knew what his favorite shirt was and that he would want to wear his big brother's Notre Dame leather jacket because he wore it all the time in life.

I knew which coffin he would like the best and he said he wanted an open coffin at the funeral so the family could "say goodbye." I picked out his favorite dragon statue, his favorite picture, and some personal effects to put out on a table for him. My mother picked out a whole bunch of pictures of him over the years for everyone to see. I also drew a cartoon for him that he always begged me to draw. It was called "cat-astrophe" and I had drawn it for him since I was in elementary school. I think he only asked me to draw it because it made me feel good. I made it so the cartoon ended for good and sobbed while I drew it. I placed the cartoon and a letter I had written for him in the casket. I don't remember what I wrote but I'm sure I repeat it every day now ... I love you and will miss you forever.

Before the wake we went to see him. He was dressed in black jeans, his favorite black t-shirt, and his Notre Dame leather jacket just like I remembered him in life. We also had his girlfriend's ring put back on his pinky (it wouldn't fit any other finger but he wore it for her all the time anyway) and we had his favorite necklaces put back on. To me, however, he looked awful. I had stared at my twin brother's face for fifteen years and this shell did not look like him. I remember the place where the bullet had entered looked the worst, but unfortunately the human body cannot be repaired after death and they did the best they could.

At the wake we stood for hours. When one so young is lost, hundreds show up to share their grief. Everyone who knew us knew how special my twin and I were. They all knew what a good person Brad was and how wonderful he was. I remember wishing that I could cry. My shock and my grief had stolen my tears from me once again.

I remember when it was finally near the end of the line I was standing near my brother's coffin just staring at him. I was screaming in my mind over and over again this can't be real, this can't be happening! Lots of people made their way through the line to pay their respects to us. It seemed like they all said the same thing over and over again. "I am so sorry for your loss" or "Condolences." What else was there to say?

A group of girls from my school who had never talked to me before stood and talked to me for a long time. They didn't say the same thing; instead they asked me questions and listened to me. It turns out those girls would be some of the closest friends I have ever had, and the fact that I am alive and sane today is due in part to them. It is funny how death lets you know who your true friends are and how well you were or are liked.

Over a thousand people attended Brad's wake. It was the biggest wake they have ever had at that funeral home to this day. My parents know so many people through their careers and every one of them knew how special their twins were to them. You could not have met either of them and not heard about their twins. With all of the people my parents knew and the fact that Brad was so young to die led so many to grieve with us that day.

At the funeral there were so many flowers and plants we could hardly fit them all next to his casket. I remember they played "Amazing Grace" because Brad told me that was his favorite Christian song, and they read John 3:16, "For God so loved the world, that he gave his only Son, that whoever believes in him should not perish but have eternal life." because he told me that was his favorite verse in the Bible. I cry every time I hear either of them to this day. I also remember wishing we could have played something by Rob Zombie or Metallica because that was more to Brad's taste. I was comforted by the fact that we had talked once about God and he said of course he believed in God and heaven and smiling when he said it.

Our family has known the funeral director for years. He was very close with my parents, and he told my mom it was the hardest funeral he had ever done. He sold that building soon after and built a new funeral parlor.

It is funny how the mind works with shock. Of all the people who came to Brad's funeral that day, I remember a man sitting in the back row the clearest. His name was Al and he was in his eighties then. He knew us through my dad's hardware store. He was sitting in the back all by himself, just sobbing. His whole body was just shaking with sobs. Brad truly affected everyone he met. It was one of the few things I remember that day. Al is now with Brad as well as both of my great-grandparents.

After that, my memory once again fast-forwards to the day we put my brother's ashes into their final resting place. I knew as unique as my brother was he should have a unique place to be in. I picked out a black sundial that could hold his ashes with two black flower canisters on both sides of it, and a plaque with his freshman year high school picture. I even wrote the saying that is on it: "Beloved Son, Twin, Brother, and Friend, Brad William Crouse November 9, 1983–May 19, 1999." Someday I vowed to build him a mausoleum that would fit his ashes and any others who wish to share my twin's final resting place, including my own ashes someday, for that was his true wish.

I did all this at fifteen.

CHAPTER TWO

SHOCK

Shock, in my opinion, is a gift. It wraps around you, dulling your senses, dulling your sense of time, and most importantly dulling your pain.

I am not exaggerating when I say that I do not remember the first year after my twin died. I functioned. I ate and drank. I even went to school and got decent grades. However, I remember none of my summer and none of my sophomore year. It is all a blank.

My shock did not end there. I remember my junior and senior years, but they are hazy and ethereal, like they happened to someone else. Someone once told me I looked like a zombie walking around. They looked in my eyes and did not see me. That is what it felt like to me as well.

Then, like most eighteen-year-olds I chose my major and my college. Both of which I left after a semester because it was the wrong choice for me. I also got married the month after my high school graduation. Talk about a life decision! Although I am very lucky and still happily married to that same man, I do not recommend anyone making any important decisions while still in shock.

Other things to not do while still in shock: I also finished college and worked for two years in a career I hated. I quit working and started a family even though I wasn't sure I was ready, just to get out of said hated career. I don't recommend doing any of that.

However, you can't avoid those decisions forever, and I feel like my shock lasted a little longer than most. In fact, I believe it took me eight or nine years to get out of shock.

I am not sure if shock can "officially" last that long, but I do know that shock is different for every person. Some remember every detail of the death, every detail of the funeral, and have no memory lapses at all. That doesn't necessarily mean you did not experience shock. Everyone is different in how he or she reacts to traumatic events. So how do you know if you experienced shock? Mostly, it is a feeling. Exhaustion and dullness are the two most common symptoms.

The reason for that is how shock affects you physically. Your body literally goes into fight-or-flight mode. All unnecessary functions of the body are shut down or minimized for the duration of your shock. This means digestion slows, breakdown of toxins and chemicals in the body slows, and your heart and lungs work harder as your body is flooded with stress hormones. Think about it this way. Fight-or-flight happens when your life is in danger. If you are running from someone who has a knife, you need more blood to pump faster so you have more oxygen to run. What you wouldn't need is that burger to be digested and the fat and chemicals from that burger to be eliminated into your liver correctly. You also wouldn't need to remember the details of that book you just read or even what you ate this morning. Well, grief and shock do the same thing. They release the same chemicals that scream to your brain, "Life in danger! Must survive!"

The problem with shock then is not only does it diminish your ability to remember, but it also makes you feel sick to your stomach and is exhausting; it actually has a very detrimental effect to your health. I believe I was in shock for eight years. That means for eight years my heart and lungs were working harder and my body was not eliminating toxins and chemicals correctly or digesting my food optimally. I suffered major health problems as a result: asthma, Graves' disease (hyperthyroid), serious migraines, and depression just to start.

Shock is helpful as long as it is temporary. I know this now. More importantly, after shock comes healing. That is essential. Not shock then more shock, then more shock for years.

So how do you "stop" shock? Good question! I do not have the answer, obviously, since it took me eight years. I can tell you right now, one of the ways I got "out of it" was to seek help—both from a doctor and from a therapist. However, there are many options when it comes to facing your grief in a healthy way.

The fact that you are reading this book tells me two things. You are a reader and you are interested in healing. So go to your library or bookstore, or fire up your e-reader and find a good book on shock, how trauma (that is what death is by the way, especially if it was a shockingly horrible death like in my story) affects you physically, etc. Find books or websites that tell you what you want to know. That will help you to find a healthy way to understand and handle your shock and grief. The second to last chapter of this book is a chapter of resources, tips, and ideas. For some resources on shock and grief feel free to go there now and look for the section labeled **Dealing With Grief**.

CHAPTER THREE

PAIN HURTS

It is a given that if I was to poke you with a needle you would feel it, say something nasty or "ow" and probably smack me if you weren't expecting it, right? So what about when something hurts not only physically but mentally as well?

Losing someone to death hurts. Many twins with whom I have spoken over the years who have lost their twins told me they actually felt something physical when their twins died. A sharp pain, a feeling like something hit them really hard in the stomach or in the chest, or even an electrical shock. I did not experience anything physical when my twin died, but boy I felt the worst pain mentally capable in a human brain.

Remember when I mentioned the tear that came out of my twin brother's eye and rolled down his cheek as my mom and I did CPR on him? Part of the reason that moment was so significant for me is that at that moment, I felt my twin leaving. More than that, I felt his emotions as he left. I felt his pain, I felt his confusion, and I felt his regret. It poured from him into me if only for as long as it took that tear to slide down his cheek. Call it a weird twin connection, call it shock, or call it whatever you want, but I had a real moment when I was connected to another person as he left his body. This has been true for the many other people I have talked to who felt something physical. Whether we like it or not, facing the death of another person hurts. For each of us who is a twin who lose a twin, amplify that one hundred times.

Death brings with it something none of us is prepared for. It brings with it a wave of feelings that bowl us over and swallows us whole. Shock dulls those feelings somewhat, but they are still there under the haze.

Each of us handles these feelings of anger, despair, helplessness, fear, and depression (as well as many others) differently. Some, like I did, run from them because we feel like we can't face them. We keep as busy as possible so we don't have a moment to stop and think about it or literally move from place to place. Some just plain deny it happened, pretending it happened to someone else. Some make up a story in their minds that those loved ones are not really dead, just out of the matrix. I did that too. Some pretend they are okay to others, bravely face the world, going back to work or school, and saying things like, "Yes, it sucks but I am okay," only to dissolve into a crumpled heap on the bathroom floor sobbing. I did that too.

Unfortunately, the pain of losing someone hurts. The sooner you face that the better. Also unfortunately, you have to face it. You cannot outrun grief. It will find you in other ways. I ran as fast as I could, but we all are forced to sleep eventually. So now I grind my teeth so hard I had to have a special mouth guard made by my dentist because I bit through the cheap ones. I have had nightmares and flashbacks for thirteen years, which I had every night for eight years. I wake up clenching my hands, my eyes, and my whole body into a ball, so tightly I have to concentrate to uncurl myself, and I ache for most of the day.

Denial does not work. That person is dead. It sucks. No matter how much we want our loved one back, he or she is not coming back.

You need to allow yourself to grieve in some way. Find some place to put it, some healthy way to handle it. But the point is you cannot escape it. You have to go low before you can go high. You have to crawl through the ditch before getting to the highway. You have to feel the needle before you get the medicine to help you. It is okay. That is normal. It is normal to feel when you hurt. It is okay to be sad. It is sad!

Don't put this book down now, however, whatever you do. It does get easier. It hurts less the more times you allow yourself to feel it. Ask anyone who has gotten allergy shots, me included (for four years!). You do eventually get used to being stabbed with a needle. It never stops hurting, but it becomes a different kind of pain—an ache instead of a sharp jab. Plus you stop anticipating it like it is something awful. It still sucks, death still sucks, but it isn't this huge beast in waiting anymore, and it doesn't feel like wrestling with said beast when you face it. Sorry, I like analogies, but you know what I mean. Face your grief in healthy doses daily. Deal with it in doses in a healthy way. Allow yourself to cry. Allow yourself to be angry, as long as it is not at yourself or other people. Be angry at that monster death. Allow yourself to hurt. Talk to people about it. Talk to those who share your grief, and if you have to or feel the need to talk to someone who can give you advice such as your pastor, a support group, a counselor, a therapist or a grief counselor—let it out!

You will be happier and healthier in the long run. I promise!

CHAPTER FOUR

HITTING BOTTOM

Sometimes grief when not handled properly leads to some of the darkest feelings we humans are capable of. Sometimes it leads to depression and even to suicidal feelings.

Over the years I have met, both in person and online, dozens of twins who have lost their twins I have figured out that one of the things we unique kind of people have in common is that we all wade through our grief for a rather specific amount of time (average six to eight years) until we hit the bottom. Now, it is not only twins who do this. Grief is so hard. It is even harder to avoid. Sometimes, either immersing ourselves into it too much or avoiding it too much consumes us. It becomes who we are instead of something we experience in healthy doses.

I often describe grieving as a wave when you are standing in the water. The first time this wave hits you it is more like a Tsunami. It will knock you over and consume you. The wave doesn't stop after the first time either. That would be too easy. Instead, the wave of grief will crash into you over and over and over again in life after losing someone to death. You go on with your life as you have to and out of nowhere get slammed with the enormous weight of grief. In the beginning, it almost always knocks you down and crushes you—hence, the crumpled person on the floor sobbing. Over time, when your grief is handled properly the wave's impact does lessen. Eventually in fact, you will be able to stay standing when that wave hits. There will come a time when you can say that person's name, see his or her picture, and even talk about that person without crying. You still will feel pain and grief of course, but you get stronger. Get that? It does not get easier, it is still the same awful wave that will never end until the day you die, but you will get stronger!

In the meantime, especially in the beginning, that wave will wash over you completely. It will knock you for a loop and immerse you in pain and agony which comes with grief. This is normal and even healthy. What is not healthy, however, is when you become so immersed in that water that there is no getting up in between the waves. There is no up. There is only down. There is no happiness or joy in your life. You are only grief. You are only sad, angry, beaten, exhausted, and in despair.

Big surprise—by not dealing with my grief properly I did this. I allowed myself to become swallowed whole by my grief. Over a period of years, eight to be exact, I slowly let the wave wear me down and pull me under until I could no longer stand.

Do you know what happened then? I sank. I sank until I no longer saw the surface of the water. I immersed myself in my grief, my pain, my shock. This is called depression.

The word depression gets thrown around a lot. Mostly from companies only interested in treating it with a pill. Remember the sad rock ad? That was always my favorite. But this is what depression feels like. There is no or very little joy or happiness. Instead, a constant down feeling that consumes your life.

At that time, I ended up having brain surgery when my children were two years and six months old (nothing to do with grief by the way; I have Arnold Chiari Malformation). Then I had the worst six-month recovery of my life.

During my recovery I was even more under the water than I was before because now I was physically exhausted as well as mentally. Usually, when you are underneath the water, so to speak, you see nothing else. You hear no one else. I know I didn't. Once again, like shock, I functioned, that was it. My children were well taken care of. In fact, I put every ounce of what I had left into caring for them. However, I was not happy. I was not experiencing the joy of raising two beautiful, healthy, happy children. I was not enjoying the quality time that I could squeeze in with my husband, family, and friends.

Eventually what happens when you are in the throes of depression is one of two things. You either fight with all your might and heal enough that you manage to get yourself back up out of it, or you do what I did, which is hit rock bottom.

You sink until you hit that point in your life that you give up. More often than not, this is when suicidal thoughts or even attempts occur. You feel hopeless. That is the biggest difference between being immersed in depression and hitting the bottom. You lose hope of ever getting back out of the water again.

For me the bottom was a moment. I hit the bottom after an exhausting shopping trip with two toddlers. I was sitting in my car. They had both fallen asleep. I was too tired to start the car, let alone drive it. Instead I sobbed. In the middle of the parking lot with my babies in the back I let it all flood out and pour over me. When I finally had it all out and had gained back enough energy to drive, I fantasized the whole way home about how to die. That is bottom. You don't get lower than that.

Time underneath the water or immersed in depression is different for every person. Some are under a long time before they hit the bottom. Others go under and straight for the bottom and sit there for a long time. Every person is different. No matter how you slice it, it is hard. Depression is very hard. It is one of the hardest things I have ever had to fight.

For me my depression lasted for about two years before I hit bottom. I struggled with postpartum depression after my oldest was born and never really stuck my head above water for very long. It was there with my daughter's first steps, her first words, my son's birth, and all of his firsts. It played havoc with my marriage and I lost a lot of friends. Depression not only affects you, but it also pulls those around you into the water, even if only temporarily.

It is also something that needs to be taken seriously. I never acted on my suicidal thoughts, thank God, but I know others who have tried. Imagine if I had? My children would have grown up without a mother, my husband without his mate, my parents would have lost another twin, and you would not be reading this book.

If you feel the feelings I have described and you feel like you may be depressed, the first step to getting better is admitting it! I had no problem with this step. I knew I was depressed, but I had no energy or hope to care. If that is where you are, do two things. Keep reading … and turn to the resources chapter right now to find some fantastic sources that helped me in the daily struggle that is depression. Look for the heading, **Healthy Ways to Deal with Depression**.

CHAPTER FIVE

FINDING THE LIGHT

There I was—submerged, feet dragging on the bottom, so depressed I could barely function and thought it might be easier just to end it all. Obviously, I am not still there. If I was, you would not be reading this. That means I got out of depression somehow.

Let me share with you something I really wished someone would have been able to get through to me when I was at the bottom. Getting out of depression only takes one step. Did you hear that? One thing! Even on my worst days of depression I could have managed one step.

After admitting you are depressed, all you have to do is push.

Back to my analogy of being on the bottom of the water, your feet touching the sand. You are cold, you are alone. You are so far in the water you cannot even see the light that is the sun, so you are also blind, deaf, and lost. By that I mean people will tell you, you are depressed. People will give you helpful and useful advice, but often you will not be able to hear them. You are so wrapped up in sadness, you yourself will not even be able to see how bad it is or how far down you have sunk. Trust me, I know.

The good news is you are not stuck. Nothing is tying you to that spot even though it may feel like it. Do you know why I am so certain? Because you are still alive! That is why. As long as you are alive you can move yourself. You can change where you are in your life.

Maybe reading this will be the push that you need. Maybe like I did, you will just plain get sick of feeling awful and think, *I don't like this anymore.* Maybe like I did, you will find someone who needs you to change (for me it was my family). Whatever it is, whatever tiny thing that gives you a tiny minute of hope, grab onto it. Focus on it. Let it build until it becomes strong enough you are ready to do that one thing I mentioned earlier.

When you are ready, push! Take your feet, gather them under you and push off of that sandy bottom. What happens? You shoot up! You may not make it out of the water right away. In fact, it will probably take several tries before you get there, depending on how deep you are, but you know what will happen? You will see the light of the sun. You will find a reason to hope. Then that one little glimpse will give you something you were missing—hope! Even if you sink to the point where you are back in the dark again you will take with you that glimpse of light, that piece of hope. Focus on it. Let it drive you until you can push even harder the next time.

For me, my push was a phone call, the hardest and scariest one I ever made. Eight years after my twin died, I called a doctor and made an appointment. I was terrified—terrified to face my grief that I had run from for so long. My hands were shaking and my voice was cracking. But in the end I figured what did I have to lose, right? I certainly could not go any lower!

After the phone call I sank back down again, of course, and was just as depressed as I was before I made that call, but now I had something that gave me hope. What if this could help me sleep without crying and screaming? What if the doctor could help me lift this constant sadness? My light was, "What if?"

Now your push doesn't have to be that same phone call. Maybe for you the right push would be to call a therapist instead (my next difficult phone call), or your pastor, or a grief support group. Maybe your push is not even a phone call, maybe it is picking up this book or another great book that can lead you in the right direction. Maybe it is an Internet search that helps you in some way. For some great ideas for a push, turn to the resources chapter under the heading **Push**.

The important thing is that you look. You search. You try. Try to find that one thing that might bring you hope. If one thing doesn't work, try something else. Trust me when I tell you it *is* that simple. Hope is one of the most powerful tools in your life.

Now push!

CHAPTER SIX

FINDING THE SURFACE

So maybe you found your push. Maybe you have not. Either way, keep trying and hang onto hope or even the idea of hope.

My first appointment with my doctor was hard. Even though I had told the receptionist when I called that my reason for my appointment was something else, I knew I had to talk to my doctor about it. When I began talking, though, I started out casually enough when the doctor asked how I was. I said I was feeling kind of down—understatement of the year. But doctors are trained for a reason. She knew there was more to it. So when she asked, I told her the truth—that I was suffering from horrible nightmares and reliving my brother's death in my sleep. That I was clenching my whole body to the point I could barely unclench my hands in the morning. That I was sad! That was the first time I heard the diagnosis of posttraumatic stress disorder (PTSD). I will get more into that later. My doctor did two things. She wrote me a prescription for an antidepressant and she highly recommended I contact a therapist. Well, I am not a big fan of medications. I never filled that prescription, but I did take her advice and called a therapist. That phone call was even harder than making an appointment with a doctor. It is hard enough to admit there is something physically wrong with you, but then to admit there is something mentally wrong? Ugh. I will admit I am a proud person, one of my many character flaws. And it was the hardest thing in the world for me to admit that I needed help. Not to mention that I lived and grew up in a very rural area my whole life. Seeing a therapist is somewhat taboo and we certainly don't talk about it. It is looked at with a kind of quiet malevolence. Like what is wrong with her that she couldn't just deal with that herself? Why does she need to "see" someone? Despite all that, I *knew* I needed to see someone and was validated by my doctor, as if I needed to be. Don't be me, by the way. Only *you* know when you need help. Only you know if you can't do it by yourself. And you know what? That is a good thing! That means you are not too proud to admit you need outside intervention. That means you get to heal!

My first appointment with my new therapist was just as hard as I thought it was going to be. By the time I actually sat down, I was ready to burst into tears just from the stress of getting to that point. In fact, I did do a lot of crying at that appointment and I had hardly scratched the surface of my grief. However, afterwards when I walked out of that office, had a real sob in the car, drove home, and went on with my day, I felt better somehow. Not quite out of my depression, of course, but like something had been lifted. Like the weight of the water holding me under wasn't nearly as heavy as it had been. Like that light I had found earlier was a little bit easier to find. Maybe even a little bit brighter.

One thing I want to mention too is that I was lucky and found the "right" therapist for me with the first phone call. Probably because I am a bit of a control freak and checked out each therapist's bio online within a twenty-mile radius of me. However, if you are uncomfortable with your therapist or you don't quite click, that is okay. It is okay to switch to a different one. Your therapist wants to help you. If that means your finding another therapist that is a better match, the better for both of you! Neither of you will be wasting your time dancing circles around your unease with each other. Once again, do not do what I did. I actually saw a grief counselor about three months after my brother's death. She was not a good fit for me to say the least. She was very young and I have a feeling I was one of her first patients. You try counseling a horribly traumatized twin teenager. I am certain it was daunting to say the least. Neither of us knew what we were doing. She did not recommend I see someone else (there's that pride again) and I just stopped seeing her after she brought up the "stages of grief" as a cop-out method of dealing with me. On a side note of my side note, please, do not ever bring up the stages of grief to someone who has lost someone to death. Especially to a teenage twin who was in shock and still thirteen years later has not gone through the stages of grief.

Now back to my story. I am not going to lie. My good feeling did not last long. I fell back into my depression pretty quickly, but I had ripped the Band-Aid™ off the wound, which was the hardest part for me. I knew what to expect now and I had already sobbed like a baby in front of a stranger. The thing was I also knew what that good feeling afterward felt like. It was hazy now, but I had a vague sense that there was something good to look forward to after my next appointment.

That is what it is like no matter what push works for you. For me and for most people it takes time. In fact it can be downright slow. That's okay. The important part is finding that light that hope, and keep finding it. Keep working at it.

For me it took two years of bobbing up and down between the light and the dark. I hit bottom a few more times when suicidal thoughts swam through me, but less and less so as time went on. Facing my grief got easier—like the needle I talked about in chapter three.

The important part is I learned how to handle all that grief and all that pain in a constructive way. For me that way was writing. In those two years I finished a memoir about my twin that I had been working on since I was fifteen. Then I kept going and began a young adult fiction series. I found my happy place and a place I could vent my grief and my sadness all at the same time.

That is what you need to do too! I don't mean writing necessarily, although it is a wonderful way to slowly get your feelings out and deal with your grief in a healthy way. In fact, most therapists will recommend you start a journal or write to the person whom you are grieving for.

If you are not a writer, that is okay; another great source I found was music. I made a CD of "mad music" that had nothing but horribly angry or sad songs that reminded me of my grief for me personally. I listened to it anytime I felt that pull back down and allowed myself a moment to feel my grief and sadness. Then when I felt like I had had enough, I turned it off and found something to make me feel happy, like watching a funny movie, going for a walk, or reading a good book. A third way I found that helped me was to find people who understand. Join a grief group; find a grief chat online or on Facebook. You can even find people who have suffered a very specific loss like from cancer or from AIDS. For me personally, I did a search and found a group that is for twins who have lost twins! You don't get much more unique than that when it comes to grief. That organization led me to meeting some whom I still consider my friends. I list some great places to start in the resources chapter under **Surface**.

You will find that each time you find something that helps that will lead to something else positive. That is how it went for me. Therapy led me to writing, which led me to pursuing getting published, which led to your reading this book! That is only one example of the hundreds of wonderful things that my life has become.

So start that journey. Keep pushing, even if it takes two years like it did me, even if it takes longer—it will happen. You will reach the surface. Like I did you will burst out of that water and feel the wonderful air on your skin. Like before, you may sink back below the surface again, but now the bounce back and wonderful feelings are even better. Now there is not only hope, but there is also relief. There is rest. There are even moments of peace. They may not last long, but like your glimpse of hope before they will each last longer and longer each time you get your head above the surface and will leave you feeling better for longer each time.

Then one day something amazing will happen. One day you will stand back up! You will be completely out of depression. That relentless wave will come back, of course. That wave will never end, and it may even knock you back under for a while. Maybe for a long while, but you will now know you can stand again. You will now have the tools to help you stand until eventually that wave may knock you down, but you will have the hope, the peace of mind, and the strength and energy to get right back up.

CHAPTER SEVEN

HOW TO KEEP YOUR HEAD ABOVE WATER

Sometimes you can be making great progress in your grief and then have something else in your life happen that slams you again. Sometimes it is another loss, sometimes it is something else traumatic, and sometimes it is something to do with your health.

I had all of these things happen since my two-year journey to the surface. I lost both of my great-grandparents whom I was very close to. I lost three grandparents. I pulled a dead baby out of a toilet (not my own, but still very traumatic), and I have had three incredibly painful surgeries since I had brain surgery.

When these things come along, make sure you spend some time dealing with them, but not dwelling on them. Don't wallow in self-pity. Most of all, don't succumb to dangerous and unhealthy ways to deal with your grief and stress. Drugs and alcohol are not a solution. In fact, they are not even a temporary fix. You know why? They are depressants. They make you feel worse. Sure, they may numb the pain, but guess what, that pain will still be there afterward and now you are more depressed and weaker when you have to face it again. Plus, drugs and even alcohol can become very addicting. This is because they are poisons. You put them in your body and your body recognizes them as poison. Then your body works very hard to get rid of it. So then the next time you go to drink or take the drug, your body remembers it from the last time and works even faster to get rid of the poison, meaning you need to consume more to feel the same effect as before. Eventually, as this vicious cycle continues, your body will "break" in some way and will still try to get rid of the poison, but the work of doing so will literally stress your organs to death. Either that or you will "need" to consume such a large amount to feel that same feeling, you will overdose. And guess what? That pain and grief will still be there until you face it in a healthy way.

Life is inevitable. Bad things are a part of life. When they come along, especially in that fragile state when you are in between depression and happiness, you have to know how to find the surface and a healthy way to stand again. Remember those good feelings you felt before. Hold onto them through the bad things. If you lose them that is okay, but make sure you try to find them again. Make sure you remember the healthy things that helped you to find them earlier. Sit down and make a list of healthy ways of making you happy if you have to. I know I have had to through my worst days.

Once you have found that place again, focus on it. Every time you get your feet back under you and stand when that wave comes, you are stronger. You are a stronger person. I know I am.

After two years, my flashbacks were gone and my nightmares were minimal. My therapist said I was at a point where therapy was no longer necessary. That meant that mentally I was doing great. Sleep free of nightmares alone will do that!

This leads me to something else important. Facing your mental pain and grief is only the first step to what all of us truly wish for—true joy. This word floated around me for years. In fact, every night I prayed for three things—peace, joy, and, happiness. This became my mantra. Peace, joy, and happiness. I want peace, joy, and happiness.

It took me awhile to figure out that what I was missing was taking care of myself physically. Don't panic. I am not jumping right to exercise or weight loss. In fact, for me I was underweight. After so many surgeries and hyperthyroid and having and nursing babies I was skeletal with a belly pooch. No, what I mean is the first step physically is the same as it is mentally. By that, I mean figuring out what is wrong with you physically.

Doing this will make it not so overwhelming to think about (I know it was for me!). Sit down and make a very depressing list of all the physical things that are either wrong with you, you would like to get rid of, or you would like to change. Mine was a long list. Now before you get too overwhelmed, pick one thing and highlight it, the thing that sticks out to you the most, the one thing that affects how you feel physically or mentally the most in a negative way. For me it was my incredibly debilitating migraines. I used to get them so bad they would knock me flat on my back for a minimum of half a day. I ended up in the hospital with them at least a couple of times a year and I would get eight to ten of them a month! Keep in mind at that time I was a stay-at-home mom who lived in the middle of nowhere with two toddlers. Help was not right around the corner.

Ok, have you listed your one thing? Now the first thing I want you to do is make another list. Write your one health problem at the top of the page and make a list of every single thing you know of that can change or improve that one thing. For me this list was short. In my life I had seen dozens of doctors and several neurologists about my migraines, the last of which told me I was "running out of options." Yours may be short too. Or it may be really long or you may need to do some research to find out what options are out there.

That is what I did. I did research. I read and read and read until my head was ready to explode. In my search, however, I found one thing that I liked the most and came across several times. For me it was not an easy fix. It was not a pill or a treatment. It was a lifestyle change. It may be the same for you or it may be what seems like an easy fix, such as medication. Just know no matter what it is there is some way to improve it even if it cannot be cured.

So the next step is to cross off the things you have tried and failed at or they did not work. I didn't even bother listing the dozens of medications I had tried. In fact, I crossed off the word medications all together. Been there, done that, hated it, didn't work. My goal was an ambitious one. My goal was to be off all prescription medications and still not get migraines.

What I found that helped me was actually pretty simple. Basically every single thing you put in your body either helps you or hurts you. There is no in-between. The thing that is not so simple about that is every person is completely unique as to what that means. We grow up learning that fruits and vegetables are good, sugar is bad. But what if someone is allergic to pineapples and strawberries? Right? So what I did was find someone who would test my unique self for the things that are good for my body and the things that are not. Turns out I am allergic to wheat. I thought, *No way*! I had eaten and cooked with whole wheat and white flour my entire life. This leads me to the other thing I learned about my health. I was not listening to my body! In fact, I felt really stupid when I stopped eating wheat and certain things went away. Every night before I went to sleep, I would have a bowl of cereal—full of wheat. Every night I was waking up to use my inhaler. Duh! By no longer eating wheat my night-time asthma improved. So simple! Well, the answer is simple anyway. Like I said earlier, switching to a wheat-free/gluten-free diet is a lifestyle change and took some time and lots of self-control, but to prove how critical something like this can be I had an anaphylactic reaction one time when I cheated and ate a crescent roll. I almost died—from a crescent roll! That is just embarrassing. On a positive note, by avoiding wheat and a few other specific things in my diet and my lifestyle, I now get maybe one migraine a month and don't even need my prescription to treat it. This is after only six months of the change! Plus, like I said before, my asthma is improved, I am off all prescriptions except my inhalers, and I have more energy than I have ever had in my life. For some resources on how to do this for yourself, turn to the chapter on resources and look under the heading, **How I Got Healthy**.

Now back to you. Do you have that one thing you highlighted and your list of things to fix it? Ask yourself two questions. Is it a temporary fix and could it lead to other problems (almost all prescription medications are on that list)? If you answered yes, that is okay to pursue it, but write next to it in permanent marker the word *temporary* in parenthesis. Temporary fixes are okay; in fact, some are absolutely necessary. If I had not used an epi-pen when I had that anaphylactic reaction, I would be dead. But that is not a permanent fix for what has now become a very serious food allergy. Instead, that temporary fix should lead to something else. For me, I am now on wheat antigen drops so I am not so lethally sensitive to wheat. What are some next steps for you? What is the permanent solution on your list? Is there one? If not, find one! Sometimes the permanent solution also happens to be a medication. If it is, thank goodness for modern medicine!

The other thing to remember is often when you pursue solving one health problem, others will be healed as well, so try not to get overwhelmed no matter how long your list is. This was very true for me. By changing my diet and seeing a naturopathic doctor about my migraines, my asthma improved, I found out some medical things I needed to pursue further, and I cured my own Grave's disease.

Also, this is not a race. There is no set date on which you have to be healthy and happy. Some will tell you to set a goal date and goal whatever. I loathe that. That only makes me feel worse when I fail to meet it. Instead, relax and enjoy your journey to a better you. Enjoy the benefits and focus on them. And above all, don't give up! It will take time. It took you how many years to get your health into the state it is. It may take years to get your health back to optimal. It took me about six months before I really began seeing benefits. It took two years before my thyroid healed. Be patient!

Finally, what I really want to relay to you is that no solution for your health problems on your list is permanent until you are comfortable in your body and healthy enough to feel peace, joy, and happiness.

Is it possible to feel those things when you are not healthy or before you get all the things crossed off your list? Of course! I am living proof. I still get migraines and I am still allergic to wheat, but

I have found my peace, my joy, and my happiness!

Just don't give up. It will take some ambition and some energy, and I know for some of us that is hard to summon up, but with every negative thing you cross off of your list, it will be more and more worth it, and you will find more and more energy and motivation to work on the next thing. Now go for it.

CHAPTER EIGHT

SETBACKS

Now some of you have already made your list, and have found a way to get to the true cause of that problem and fix it. Awesome! Keep it up!

For most of us, however, that is harder than it sounds. When I made my list, I was out of my underwater depression faze, but that may not be the case for some of you. For some of you, in fact, you may even still be on the bottom and not even able to see the light yet. That is okay! In fact, it is never too early to get started on improving your life. Today is the day. Make that first step I talked about earlier. Sometimes treating yourself physically may be the thing that will lead to healing mentally.

The reason for that is the one major thing that I haven't mentioned yet that affects each one of us daily: stress. One of the definitions of stress from Meriam-Webster.com is: "a physical, chemical, or emotional factor that causes bodily or mental tension and may be a factor in disease causation." So if you are physically unhealthy, depressed, and are facing a death of someone you know, you have physical, chemical, and emotional factors that may cause disease. That is why I emphasize working on getting out of the depression first. Especially since depression is such a huge chemical and emotional weight that it truly does affect everything in your daily living. It *is* a disease and it *causes* disease by building up stress in your body. If you feel that working on something on your list will also help with your depression, more power to you! Start there. Just get started.

Okay, back to stress. How does stress affect your body? Everyone knows stress is bad. It makes you sick. It causes disease. We all try to get rid of stress. But why? The reason is exactly like shock and grief that I mentioned earlier. Stress puts out chemicals from your brain that put you in fight-or-flight mode. It makes your heart work harder for no reason (you are not in immediate danger), it makes your digestion work poorly, and it makes your body inefficient at filtering out toxins such as carbon dioxide, chemicals, and bile from your liver. These toxins build up in your bloodstream and get circulated throughout your body, poisoning your organs, your cells, and even your brain. Then your body reacts to the toxins and tries to heal itself, which it is perfectly capable of. However, more stress pours more toxins in right behind the last batch of toxins, overwhelming your body once again. It is a vicious and ugly cycle.

The other thing to consider is what causes us stress. Automatically I say stress and you think, bad things, such as the car won't start, but that is actually not the case. In fact, according to this graph on the Holmes and Rahe stress scale from Wikipedia, good things that cause stress in our lives, like getting married, can cause just as much if not more stress than the bad things!

Life event	Life change units
Death of a spouse	100
Divorce	73
Marital separation	65
Imprisonment	63
Death of a close family member	63
Personal injury or illness	53
Marriage	50
Dismissal from work	47
Marital reconciliation	45
Retirement	45
Change in health of family member	44
Pregnancy	40
Sexual difficulties	39
Gain a new family member	39

Business readjustment	39
Change in financial state	38
Death of a close friend	37
Change to different line of work	36
Change in frequency of arguments	35
Major mortgage	32
Foreclosure of mortgage or loan	30
Change in responsibilities at work	29
Child leaving home	29
Trouble with in-laws	29
Outstanding personal achievement	28
Spouse starts or stops work	26
Begin or end school	26
Change in living conditions	25
Revision of personal habits	24
Trouble with boss	23
Change in working hours or conditions	20
Change in residence	20
Change in schools	20
Change in recreation	19
Change in church activities	19
Change in social activities	18
Minor mortgage or loan	17
Change in sleeping habits	16
Change in number of family reunions	15
Change in eating habits	15
Vacation	13
Christmas	12
Minor violation of law	11

Score of 300+: At risk of illness.
Score <150: Only have a slight risk of illness.

In addition to what kinds of stress we are exposed to, you also have to consider that each one of us reacts to stress differently. I am a pretty laid-back person, but I am also extremely sensitive to stress. I do not watch the news because it gives me nightmares. Any cruelty to animals affects me so much it bothers me years after I see it. I once accidentally watched a video of someone skinning an animal alive to make fur boots and it still wakes me up, makes me sick, and makes me cry years later! I also get my feelings hurt very easily. My stress reaction is so extreme; in fact, I have been diagnosed with two stress-related disorders. I was diagnosed with Post Traumatic Stress Disorder (PTSD) from my twin brother's death, which means my body is in a constant state of extreme stress all the time and reacts to "triggers" of that event in an extreme way. I also am a "highly sensitive person" or HSP. For more info on what either of these mean, check out the resource chapter and look under **PTSD** or **HSP**.

However, some people are the opposite of me. They get "sappy" about nothing, no one can hurt their feelings, and they thrive on stories of torture, horror, and bad news. They will react very differently to stress than I will! If you don't know which one you are, it may be helpful to do some self-evaluation. Pay attention to how you feel when stressed. What stresses you out? Are you a "sensitive" person, a deep thinker or not?

The hard thing is that often things that cause us stress are really just necessary evils. Driving can be stressful but necessary. Caring for a baby is necessary and essential but can be overwhelmingly stressful. Then we add in things that make our lives easier or more entertaining but which also cause stress— such as the six "I-whatever" devices we all carry around.

Take for example a new digital camera. It is a great thing to own and use. The pictures are worth every penny. But now you have the stress of figuring out how to use it, the stress of getting that great shot (ever tried taking a picture of a toddler?), and then the stress of downloading the pictures, ordering them, paying for them, and putting them into albums or picture frames. Finally, did you remember to charge the camera? In other words, no one can avoid stress. Even if we were perfectly healthy, never had to face grief, and were in a total state of constant happiness, stress would still find us!

So what can you do about it? Two things.
1. <u>Avoid It</u>
2. <u>Manage it</u>

You can take this one step further as well by looking a little closer at the thing that is causing you stress. Think about it a little harder. When something is stressing you out, evaluate it. Look at it with an investigative approach. Ask yourself some who, what, why, when, where, how, and why questions that may seem obvious, but will make you feel better when you get the answers.

Ask: How can I figure this out? Why is this causing me stress? What can I do to make it less stressful? Where can I go to make it less stressful? Who can help me make this less stressful? Etc. With practice you will soon be doing this automatically and coming up with a much less stressful alternative all the time.

How can you manage it? I have one word for you: organize! I am sure some of you are cringing already, but seriously the number one thing a psychologist will tell you to do to manage your stress is to organize it. One thing you need to know about me is that I am a type A, control freak, organizer. Look out! But that is how I handle stress. At this point in my life I am a stay-at-home mom to a six-year-old and four-year-old, I home school, I run the house and pay all the bills, I work part time out of my home, I am an author of one book and working on writing several more, and I volunteer at my church about five hours a week. In other words, I am busy! The only reason I manage to "do it all" so to speak, is I am painfully organized. I don't mean my schedule by the way. I have two little children; schedules rarely work around here because everyone who has them knows that children are unpredictable little messes waiting to interrupt you, coerce you into a game, spill their milk on the floor, and are constantly looking for something to eat. What I do mean is my house is organized. My calendar is organized. My paperwork is organized. My "school" is organized.

Etc. I take one task at a time throughout my day and I organize it in the most time-efficient, neatest, easiest way possible. Do I still have the stress of all of those things I do? Of course, but it is now organized stress which makes me feel better. This is what is important. If it makes you feel better or less stressed, you are organizing. It doesn't have to mean having a place for every toy or socks neatly in a row by color, because for some people that is more stressful. Trust me; I grew up with a mother who loathes organization. To her, throwing all of her hundreds of fabrics onto a table in a pile makes her feel good. It drove me insane, but to her it makes sense and makes her feel less stressed. So to her that is organization. Whatever makes you feel less stressed is okay.

The final way to deal with stress is by eliminating it. Most of us are so stressed and so exhausted from that stress that we literally do not have the energy at the end of the day to either manage or eliminate the stress we have built up throughout the day. I know; I have been there. That is why I am going to be honest and tell you this is the hardest part, but also worth the most. I will explain.

I used to be a basket case by the time my husband got home from work. My nerves were shot, my patience was gone, and my energy was a memory from that morning. I was exhausted! With that came the emotions that go with someone who is too stressed, pushing too hard, and burning out. In other words, I was really crabby, to say it nicely. I snapped at the littlest things the kids did, I exploded when they didn't listen, and I was too tired to even have a meaningful conversation with my husband, let alone any quality time. At one point, I was so overwhelmed and stressed it became a daily, then weekly, then monthly thing that ended up pulling me back under the water. I was depressed. Naturally, I lashed out at everyone and everything around me. Because it had to be everyone else's fault. The kids are brats, my husband isn't doing enough, people keep taking advantage of me, etc., etc. You know what? That was all true. Ha! My kids could be naughty, my husband could have helped me more, and people did take advantage of me, but here is the thing that I learned. I was the one letting all of those things bother me. Sounds simple, right? Nope. It took me two years to figure it out and allow myself to stop blaming others and look at myself honestly. So eventually, I learned to not let the kids' behavior stress me out so much. I learned to appreciate the things my husband did do and learned how to ask when I really needed more help with something. I learned how to say no! I am a total people pleaser. This was very hard for me, but after the first couple times of saying it, the people who were the worst about it stopped asking me!

Secondly, it means working very hard at changing yourself. Did I mention I am a huge perfectionist who hates admitting when I am wrong? It took me two years! You know what though? I did it a little bit at a time every day.

Then one day one of my children spilled his milk and I stopped, took a deep breath, and thought to myself, is it going to change the fact that I still have to clean up a mess if I freak out or yell? No. I will still have to clean up a mess. So instead, I hugged my child who was bracing himself for the wrath of mean mommy monster and asked if he could help me clean it up. He was so relieved and now every time he spills, he asks to help clean it up. Ta-dah! Less stress

The last thing I want to mention is that there are a million things out there to help you deal with stress in a healthy way. Herbs, supplements, medications (as a last resort), meditations, exercise routines, yoga routines, etc.

I will not lecture you with the same old thing I hear and read constantly; exercise is the best way to deal with stress. All that did with me was to make me dig in my heels, pout like a little girl, and say no, I don't wanna! Then I felt guilty when I didn't.

As far as exercise, I am not a big exercise person. I know I should at least walk every day or something, but I have no urge to do so. None. However, I recently tried yoga for the first time from the comfort of my living room and I fell in love. It is something I feel good while doing it, look forward to the next time I get to do it, does not harm me in any way, and it actually helps reduce stress! I found my winner.

Yoga may not be for you. That is okay, but the important thing for you to do is to start looking and experimenting with something that is your thing. I have a great list of suggestions in the resources chapter, under **Healthy Ways to Deal with Stress**, to get you started. Still didn't find one? Look online! Ask around. Just don't give up, and keep on trying.

CHAPTER NINE

DEATH PREPAREDNESS

Picture this. Here I was fifteen, just finishing up my freshman year of high school. Excited about summer coming soon. Excited about new friends I had made. Excited about my first job away from the family farm. Excited about life. Like I can imagine most fifteen-year-olds are. This in reality is how most of us are when death comes to find us. We are walking along, living our lives, focused on the things we find important to that stage of life, trying to be happy.

Then *bam*! Someone dies—a close family member, a friend, a partner, etc. Then we wonder why no one had ever talked to us about this thing called death. Why had no one ever prepared us? In fact, why don't we as a culture talk about death?

I of course knew what death was. I had known people who had died. I had been to a funeral. Lost lots of pets. In fact, I had talked in depth with my twin about death. We were going to be getting our driver's licenses soon and we were asking each other if the other one would be donating their organs. That discussion led to another about how the other would like to be buried. That discussion led to one about losing each other—as it goes with twins.

Still, did I expect my twin to be dead two weeks after that discussion? Of course not! In fact, I don't think it is possible to prepare yourself for a loss. I have spoken to dozens of people who have lost their loved ones to disease or cancer, which many times was a long drawn-out journey. Their loss, although different from mine, was no less prepared for. No less comforting. No less easy to bear.

Can you be truly prepared for death to enter into your life? My answer is no. That sucks I know. However, you can do something right now to help with this. If you have children, talk to them about it. Now, stay age appropriate of course. Your five-year-old does not need to know that Mommy could get hit by a bus tomorrow. But bring it up. When you find a dead bird, don't just say it is sleeping. Say it is dead. It is in bird heaven. It is in a better place. Describe that place. We are Christians, so we believe in heaven. That may not be the case in your house, but whatever you believe, share it with your kids. It annoys me that death is something we hear nothing about until we are forced to be at a funeral. Especially when it is inevitable!

My kids have their own heaven all picked out. Castles, kitty rooms, trains, etc., all custom fit for them. So now when someone dies that they know (which is inevitable) death won't be this obtuse, scary unknown.

Will it still hurt? Of course! Death hurts. Talk about that with them too!

Ok, so you don't have kids? That is fine. Talk to your friends and family. I know—depressing conversation alert. But it is not as depressing as experiencing your mom's death and having no idea what she wanted. There are a lot of decisions to make when someone dies. I made most of them at fifteen for my twin brother. Why? Because we had just talked about all of them a week before he died. I knew his final wishes. I gave him exactly what he asked for. Did it make his loss easier? No! However, looking back now it gives me a sense of peace about his funeral and that we donated his organs, and that he was cremated. All these were his wishes, coming directly from him, in his own words.

Finally, plan for your own death. Make it easy on those who will be dealing with your loss. Meet with a lawyer, now, to complete a will. Yes, I know a lawyer is not necessary but it makes your will the most official by law that your wishes will be honored. Trust me, it is worth the money. If you are not an adult yet talk to your parents about it.

Secondly, put in writing your final wishes. Answer the questions that need answering. Do you want to be buried or cremated? Do you want your ashes put someplace specific or kept on a mantel somewhere? Do you want a funeral? Where? Do you want a casket or just your ashes shown at your funeral? Do you want an open or closed casket? What do you want to wear as your final outfit? All these questions are just about your body and are not a complete list. Then there is your burial plot, your headstone, and all the details of your funeral.

After that there is your money, your debts, your possessions, your home, etc. What do you want done with all of them? See why I mentioned meeting with a lawyer or talking to your parents in advance. They will help you think of all the questions that need to be answered. They will make it much easier than tackling it on your own.

If you are dead set against meeting with anyone, explore your library or bookstore. There are several books out there that can help you get organized and make some tough choices while they are still your choices to make. I will have a list of some in my chapter on resources under the title **Death Preparedness**.

Planning for death sounds morbid or worse like you are ready for it, but that is not my intention at all. It is a responsible thing to do. Please do not take this chapter as an invitation to end your life or give up on living. Life after losing someone is hard, but never without hope. Remember that. Suicide is not a solution! It does not solve your problems. It is creating a problem for everyone who ever knew you. Especially those who love you or are the closest to you. Don't turn to suicide, turn to hope that you will heal and you will even be happy again.

CHAPTER TEN

WHAT PEACE, JOY, AND HAPPINESS FEEL LIKE

Little by little, day by day, I have built my life into something that brings me peace, joy, and happiness. How do I know I am happy? Because I want more of the same that I have—more of the same feelings, more of the same days, more of the same moments.

What is peace? Honestly, peace is feeling good, despite the bad. Grief is awful and there are things in life that are really hard on top of grief. Finding peace is being okay, despite life and despite grief. How do I know I have peace? Because I enjoy each of those things almost all of the time. I enjoy the feelings I am flooded with now. I enjoy my days and I enjoy the many moments that make up my day.

Finally, joy. Oh man, joy is something I have sought for so long. You know you can always tell when a person is full of joy. They are the people who you just love to be around. You love to listen to them. You love to spend time with them. They make you feel good just by being near them. You know whom I am talking about. Although I am modest and I am not sure anyone would love to be around me constantly, there are times now when I want to be around me. Ha! That's right, when you experience joy, you actually like yourself. You like how you feel. You like how you make others feel. You like who you are and you like the things that you do. That is ultimate joy right there.

In my life I feel those things most of the time now. Of course there is still that wave in my life, that wave of grief that crashes into me. The thing is, though, that wave feels a lot less powerful. This isn't true of course. The horrific loss of my twin brother is no less awful. The world is no less robbed of him, and I miss him just as much every single day as I did the day he died. However, I am so much stronger than I was so many years ago. That wave keeps coming, but it almost never knocks me down now. Or if it does, I get right back up. I never thought I would be able to say that. Through my shock, my grief, my depression, my health problems, my stress, I thought my grief would always drown me; that I would never be able to talk about him or his death without losing it completely. In the beginning that is true, you can't. It hurts too much and you are not strong enough yet. But the thing to remember is <u>you will be</u>.

Then when you are, you will have the honor of sharing the person you lost with the world like I do. You will *get* to talk about that special person in fondness. You will have the joy of remembering the wonderful memories you made with that person. You get to share how much this person affected those around him or her in such powerful ways. In my case, I get to talk about the fact that I grew up with a twin, had an awesome childhood as a twin. How special is that? I get the honor of teaching my children about Brad. How great "Uncle Curly" truly was and how much he meant to me.

Hang in there. Feel the pain. Grieve. Then get back up and keep going. Be relentless in your pursuit of peace, joy, and happiness. I promise you, you will find them. If I can after all I have been through, so can you!

CHAPTER ELEVEN

GET STARTED!

One thing I have learned through my journey is that all good in my life has brought more good. It is the best-kept secret in the world. Good attracts good and bad attracts bad. Once I found my light, I held onto it for dear life. I focused on it. I fantasized about it. I dreamed about it. I immersed myself in it. Then you know what happened? It grew into something more, something even better, and something that lasted longer and made me feel even better. Then things around me started to get better. It is that simple. Find one good thing. Grab onto it. Focus on having it. It will bring you more good things.

Life is truly what we make it. If you lose someone, feel that awful inevitable pain, and focus on it for too hard and too long, it will suck you into it for as long as you let it. I did that myself. I know it can be so hard to *not* focus on it. You feel guilty for not focusing on that loss. You feel bad for feeling happiness when that person you love is not here to enjoy it with you. You may even feel guilty for being alive when that person is not. I felt those things for a long time. In fact, I still feel those feelings. However, I do not focus on them, dwell in them, or sink myself with them. I feel them then mentally shift myself to feel something else, like the way my brother got the attention of everybody just by his mere presence when he walked into a room. I switch my negative thoughts and feelings to something that makes me feel good. One thing that helped me a lot in doing this was making a list of things that would automatically make me smile or laugh. For instance, the way my daughter throws her head back when she laughs. The way my son laughs so hard he falls on the floor sometimes. That intense look full of love my husband gives me when I am doing the most mundane things, like washing the dishes. Even the contented mush my cat becomes when I pet her belly. You don't have to write your list down if you don't want to, but search through your life and find these things that bring you instant happiness. Even if they only last for a moment, focus on them whenever you feel sad or down. Bring yourself back up.

Better yet, *do* things that bring you happiness. Watch movies and shows that lift your mood, make you feel good, or make you laugh. Read books or even funnies that bring you joy and make you laugh. Go to places that you love. Can't afford to go to the place you believe will bring you happiness? Go there virtually online with pictures of it or through a book or through a movie about it. Heck, go there in your mind!

This brings me to another thing that has literally saved my life. Right now, after you read this of course, close your eyes. Think about a place in your life that has brought you a huge amount of happiness or joy. If you had a horrible childhood or can't think of one make one up that you wished you could go to—a beach, in the middle of the woods, a park. Wherever. Just pick a place you can feel safe and at peace in. Now go there in your mind. Close your eyes and allow yourself to be there. Smell the smells. Hear the sounds. Feel the feelings that make it great. Focus on it until you literally smile or get tears of peace in your eyes.

One of my happy places was on top of a barn roof. No kidding. I used to climb up onto this roof with a book and read. I loved the feeling of the sun shining on my face, the wind rustling my hair, the smell of the woods near our barn lightly drifting over me. Most of all, I loved the feeling of being on top of the world, away from it all. No one knew about my secret place to read and this made me feel even more powerful. It was my secret hiding place. I loved it.

Every time I have had to face something particularly awful I go back to that place. After a really bad sobbing fest, when I would be lying in a heap on the floor, my tears of grief finally letting me go, I would go, back to the roof, hear the wind, and feel the sun. It calmed me down. It got me back to normal. It helped me get back to my life feeling better. Another example is the many MRIs I had to have before and after my brain surgery. I am claustrophobic, especially when something is touching my head. For the many MRIs I had they strapped my head into a vice, strapped me to a table and stuffed me into a tube where the surface was inches from my face, my arms, and my back for hours. Just thinking about it makes me panic. I got through it without sedation by going to my happy places. I have more than one and found many more in that tube. But I did it. I stayed calm. I did not panic. In fact, when I finally got out I was okay. Glad it was over, but okay.

Now it is your turn. Find your place and use it. You will be amazed at how simple and how wonderful it will make you feel, even in the worst moments of your life. I have suggestions for **Happy Places** and **Instant Happiness Triggers** in the resources chapter.

Death sucks. Grieving is the hardest thing you will ever do. But you know what? After facing it, everything else that you do will seem easy. Life will seem easier, because you will be able to say, *well, if I can get through losing someone whom I cared about that much, then a job interview is nothing*. Or facing a surgery. Or public speaking. Or even losing someone else. They will all seem less scary and less awful. You know why? Not because they are, but once again because you are that much stronger.

My only hope, my only wish is that by reading this you will want to try. You will find the glimmer of hope that you need to take you to your next step toward a better life for you. If you take nothing else from reading this book, at least take that from me. Take hope. You can do this. You can get through this. You will be okay. And if you let yourself, you will be more than okay. You will find happiness again. You will find peace.

Death is inevitable, unavoidable, and hard, and life can be too, especially when facing grief. But life can also be wonderful. It can also be exciting. It can also be something you look forward to and something you never want to end. All it takes is one thing, one decision to want to be happy. You can be happy and you will.

CHAPTER TWELVE

RESOURCES

Throughout the book I mention this chapter many times. You may have skipped right here and that is okay too. This chapter is full of ideas, sources, and places to help you get through your grief, to come out of your depression, and to improve your life.

This is not a complete list. If you feel like there is something I missed that particularly helped you and you would like to share it with me, thank you! You can find a link on my website: Breasbooks.com that says Contact. You will also find additional resources on my website and on my Facebook page which you can find here: https://www.facebook.com/#!/pages/Death-Sucks-Life-Doesnt-Have-To/138759956298358?fref=ts

You can also find my page on Facebook by typing in Death Sucks, Life Doesn't Have To, in the search section.

Please note these are my opinions and my suggestions, and not of the authors of the books or websites I mention. Also, I am in no way a professional in the field of trauma or recovery. I am just someone who has been through my own grief and through my own experience who wishes to help others form what I have learned by experiencing it. Always seek a professional in all medical, lifestyle or health changes or decisions.

I hope that through this book and these resources you will find some comfort and peace that will help you through the hardest thing in your life you will ever do. I hope you will find the strength to improve your life in every way and find peace, joy, and happiness once again.

Resources

Brad William Crouse

This book would not be complete for me if I did not share some of my twin with you. For the full story of his death and who he was check out my website listed above and click on the tab that says Blog. Additionally, if you are a twin who has lost a twin or know one, you will find some great links to organizations that will connect you with others like me who have lost a twin. Look for the miscellaneous resources at the end of this chapter.

Dealing with Grief
*Resources to help you deal with grief in a healthy way
- Books
1. *ABC's of Healthy Grieving: A Companion for Everyday Coping* by Harold Ivan Smith
2. *How To Go On Living When Someone You Love Dies* by Therese A. Rando
3. *Grieving with Hope: Finding Comfort as You Journey through Loss* by Samuel J IV Hodges
4. *Grieving: A Beginner's Guide* by Jerusha Hull McCormack
5. *Healing Your Grieving Heart for Teens: 100 Practical Ideas (Healing Your Grieving Heart series)* by Alan D. Wolfelt PhD
6. *I Wasn't Ready to Say Goodbye: Surviving, Coping and Healing after the Sudden Death of a Loved One* by Brook Noel
7. *We Are All in Shock: How Overwhelming Experiences Shatter You ... And What You Can Do About It* by Stephanie Mines

There are hundreds more. Do an online search. Explore your library. Find the one that speaks the most to you and works the best for you!

- <u>Websites</u>
1. http://helpguide.org/mental/grief_loss.htm
Loss of a spouse:
2. www.aarp.org/family/lifeafterloss
Loss to cancer, but also lists some symptoms and feelings of grief:
3. http://www.cancer.org/treatment/treatmentsandsi deeffects/emotionalsideeffects/griefandloss/coping -with-the-loss-of-a-loved_one-intro-to-grief-mourning-bereavement
This one shows you how to help someone who is grieving and also has a great list of unhealthy versus healthy ways to grieve:
4. http://www.simplesympathy.com/grieving-process.html
This shows how to grieve properly, especially as a family:
5. http://sfhelp.org/grief/policy.htm
Good site for teens and talking to teens about grieving:
6. http://kidshealth.org/teen/your_mind/emotions/so meone_died.html
A good site for teens and sudden losses:
7. http://www.hellogrief.org/

When Someone Dies
*The funeral, their will, their final wishes
- Books
1. Written by a lawyer who made some costly and regretful mistakes when his mother died: *When Someone Dies: The Practical Guide to the Logistics of Death* by Scott Taylor Smith, Michael Castleman
2. *What to Do before and after Someone Dies: A Practical Guide to Help You through the Worst Possible Time for Making Important Decisions* by Judith Ellen Lee

*Helping others to deal with loss and grieving
- Books
1. *Being There For Someone In Grief - Essential Lessons for Supporting Someone Grieving From Death, Loss and Trauma* by Marianna Cacciatore
2. *When Someone Very Special Dies: Children Can Learn to Cope with Grief (Drawing Out Feelings Series)* by Marge Heegaard
3. *How Do We Tell the Children? A Step-by-Step Guide for Helping Children Two to Teen Cope When Someone Dies* by Dan Schaefer
4. A picture book for young kids: *I Miss You: A First Look At Death* by Pat Thomas

- <u>Websites</u>
1. http://www.helpguide.org/mental/helping_grieving.htm
2. Some short and simple tips: http://www.cancercare.org/publications/67 how_to_help_someone_who_is_grieving
3. Emphasis on men's grief: http://griefwords.com/index.cgi? action=page&page=articles %2Fhelping11.html&site_id=3

Support Groups
*All kinds of loss
-Online
1. http://www.griefwatch.com/support-group
2. http://www.griefshare.org/
3. http://grief.supportgroups.com/
4. http://www.dailystrength.org/c/Bereavement/support-group
5. http://www.griefnet.org/

-Organizations

1. The Compassionate Friends is a national, non-profit network for bereaved parents and siblings. www.compassionatefriends.org
2. The National Alliance for Grieving Children – offers a center locator which can connect families with support in their community. www.nationalallianceforgrievingchildren.org
3. Men's Bereavement Network for surviving spouses. www.mensbereavement.org

*Death to Cancer
1. An online support group for all losses, but an emphasis on loss to cancer: http://www.onlinegriefsupport.com/group/losings omeonetocancer
2. A site dedicated to losing someone to cancer support groups: http://www.cancercare.org/tagged/grief_and_loss

Healthy Ways to Deal with Depression
- Books
1. *The Mindfulness and Acceptance Workbook for Depression: Using Acceptance and Commitment Therapy to Move Through Depression and Create a Life Worth Living (New Harbinger Self-Help Workbook)* by Patricia J. Robinson
2. *The Mindful Way through Depression: Freeing Yourself from Chronic Unhappiness* by Mark Williams
3. *Depression: The Way Out of Your Prison* by Dorothy Rowe
4. *The 10 Best-Ever Depression Management Techniques: Understanding How Your Brain Makes You Depressed and What You Can Do to Change It* by Margaret Wehrenberg

- Websites

1. Great site for self-help and motivation tips: http://www.helpguide.org/mental/depression_tips.htm
2. This site is very specific and talks about all kinds of depression and natural herbs/supplements and tips to help deal with it. http://www.depressionhelpfiles.com/articles/a1.htm
3. This is a very specific and extensive article on natural ways to treat depression. http://www.naturalhealthweb.com/articles/weil2.html

Suicide Prevention
Call the National **Suicide Prevention** Lifeline at 1-800-273-8255
http://www.suicidepreventionlifeline.org/

- Websites
1. The American Foundation for Suicide Prevention: http://www.afsp.org/
2. Excellent website about loss, depression, and suicide prevention: http://www.save.org/
3. Suicide prevention, awareness and support: http://www.suicide.org/index.html
4. A website from suicide survivors' perspectives: http://www.suicidology.org/home

- Books
1. *How I Stayed Alive When My Brain Was Trying to Kill Me: One Person's Guide to Suicide Prevention* by Susan Rose Blauner
2. *Hello Cruel World: 101 Alternatives to Suicide for Teens, Freaks and Other Outlaws* by Kate Bornstein
3. *Step Back from the Exit: 45 Reasons to Say No to Suicide* by Jillayne Arena

4. *Suicide: The Forever Decision* by Paul G. Quinnett

Push/Surface

There are many things that can be your first step towards healing. Some of them are easy and you will wonder why you hadn't done them earlier. Some are hard, but sometimes it takes work and strength in a time in your life when you feel like you have neither in you (but you do!). I will list some places to find some of the things that worked for me. If you don't find one that works for you, keep searching! Take a look at the following section labeled **Surface** for some other ideas and section above labeled **Support Groups**. Anything that brings you a little piece of hope counts!

- Websites
1. This site is an easy way to search for a therapist or counselor in your area:
   http://www.networktherapy.com/directory/find_therapist.asp
2. Good page about grief counseling and how to find the right counselor:
   http://www.allaboutcounseling.com/dir/grief-counseling/
3. You can also do a specific search on any search engine, such as grief counselor in Green Bay, Wisconsin, and that will almost always bring up a list in or near your area.

Surface/Push

I talk about breaking above the surface of the water that is depression in chapter six, "Finding the Surface." These are suggestions of ways to handle grief and pain in a constructive way and go right along with **Push** in the section before this one.

1. Read. You never know when someone else's words are going to change your life and be the encouragement you need to take that next step to

change your life for the better.

2. Music can be a powerful tool which can have the same potential effect as reading someone else's words.

3. Writing may be the thing that helps you catch a glimpse of something you need to help yourself heal. Write a letter to those you lost. Write to a friend or family member. Write a book about your loss. Write poetry. Put your hands to a keyboard or a pencil to a paper and see what comes out.

4. Make a phone call like I did. Call a therapist. Call a counselor. Call your doctor to help you deal with it and/or help you find a grief counselor or therapist. Call your religious advisor for counseling and advice. Call your parents. Call your friends who knew that person you lost and are probably feeling their loss as well. What do you have to lose?

5. Start a new hobby—something you have always wanted to do, but never did. It may be the little light in your week that gives you the hope you need. The Internet has a plethora of resources for anything you may want to start. Some suggestions are geocaching, which is like a treasure hunt with your GPS. Buy a metal detector and walk the beach. Start a new collection in memory of the someone you lost (I continued my brother's shot glass collection).
Here is a fun website for more ideas:
http://www.findmeahobby.com/.

6. Learn something new. We all have things we always wanted to take a class on or hire someone to teach us to do. A new language. How to play an instrument. A dance class. To crochet or knit. How to use computers. The opportunities are endless. Check your local library's bulletin board or call them for free classes offered in your area. Call a college near you or check out their website to see what classes

they are offering for free or are reasonably priced. Look in the newspaper under services offered. Opportunities for online classes and courses on every subject can be found as well.

7. Join a support group for loss or your specific kind of loss. You can find some great ways to find one in this chapter under the section labeled **Support Groups**. You can also call your local hospital and do an online search. Sometimes speaking with someone or a group who understands what you are going through can be that little piece of hope as you heal together.

8. Volunteer. Sometimes helping can lead to healing. Volunteering gives you a purpose to get out of the house. It gives you meaning to your day. It makes you feel good to help others. You can help others anytime. Help your neighbor carry groceries in. When someone drops papers, help pick them up. Offer to babysit. If you want a bigger challenge, call the nursing homes or assisted living facilities in your area. They are always in need of volunteers. Call a hospital near you. Not a people person? Call your local animal shelter. Playing with a cat or walking a dog may just make your day. Check out this great website for some more suggestions in your area: http://www.volunteermatch.org/.

    Search the internet for many more ideas!

9. Adopt a pet. If you feel like you are capable of the responsibilities of pet ownership, pets have so many benefits! They give you something to focus on besides your loss. They depend on you completely, which gives you a sense of meaning and purpose. They give love when you need it the most! They help you to feel less lonely. They listen without judgment or giving you a sense of guilt. They make you laugh every day.

10. Find your own push that can bring you just a little

bit of hope that life after loss is worth living. That there are good things in the world. Things to look forward to, that give you the hope that it is going to get easier, and more importantly, you are going to get stronger and get through this!

How I Got Healthy

The thing we need to learn as a society when it comes to our health is that each one of us is unique. How we got to the way our health is now is unique. How those things have affected us is unique. You could group ten people together who all have the same exact ailment and every single one of them would have different symptoms, different results from the same treatment, and different effects emotionally.

So the trick is to find someone (or several different people) willing to look at you specifically from birth until now. The other side of that coin is to stay as close to natural as possible. Instead of feeding your body more chemicals which your body often treats like a poison and tries to get rid of it as quickly as possible working your filtration system, lymph system, and immune system much harder than it should be, consider using natural cures and treatments. That is what I set out to do. However, I got completely overwhelmed with the loads of vitamins and supplements available today. Searching the internet made it even worse.

So what I did was go see a naturopathic doctor. I was tired of trying drug after drug with so many side effects only to hear them tell me I was about out of options. Basically, a naturopathic doctor treats like with like and uses all natural things found in nature to treat you.

A naturopathic doctor will figure out how you got to the point you are at with your health, what needs to be improved, and then find the best way to treat what needs to be fixed, sometimes utilizing physical, mental, and even spiritual treatments combined. They look at you specifically as a person and your needs. They treat all of you as naturally as possible.

The first thing my naturopathic doctor did was get my

extensive background (and reviewed my stack of medical records before I came). Then he examined me and did several blood and urine tests to see where I was in several different areas he suspected were causing my health problems. Then at my next appointment he laid out a plan of action to treat me according to my test results in the most specific way possible. What I was seeing him for was asthma, allergies, Graves' disease (hyperthyroid), and severely debilitating migraines. In my case it was discovered I am allergic to wheat, which I found out is common when you have thyroid issues. If you want more information on why that is, Google it. Just by eliminating wheat in my diet, in only three months my asthma had improved and my migraines had all but disappeared. To show you how amazing that is, I tried over a dozen medications to try to prevent and treat my migraines! This goes to show you that medicine should pay attention to you as an individual.

Now in my opinion there is no such thing as one way to treat one person. My doctor agrees. Traditional medicine has its purpose and its place as well. Chiari malformation is a genetic defect of the skull. No amount of natural treatments will cure the underlying problem, and in my case I would be dead without traditional medicine. My brain was forgetting to breathe at random times and I literally had to consciously remember to breathe again. During the day it was scary; at night I was not conscious, so I could not tell myself to breathe again. Soon I became terrified to sleep. It got worse and worse until I stopped breathing for so long I had a seizure in my sleep. I may have had many others I was unaware of, but this particular seizure was bad enough it actually realigned my jaw. Without surgery it would have continued to get worse. I would most likely have died of a seizure or at best been blind (Chiari damaged my eyes) and paralyzed, which sometimes happens with severe Chiari that is left untreated. So in that case traditional medicine saved my life.

Another example is as a result of my Chiari (and lying flat on my back for six weeks after surgery) the bones in my neck were seriously out of alignment. So once again my naturopathic doctor referred me to a chiropractor who has treated me wonderfully and played a big part in preventing my migraines.

The important thing to remember is that you are an individual with individual, specific health concerns. Each one may require a different person treating it. A truly wonderful naturopathic or holistic doctor like mine will realize that and utilize all the tools and resources necessary to treat you individually.

Another similar option is a holistic doctor. Holistic doctors, according to Holistichelp.net, "... are educated and trained in traditional medicine and hold a medical degree. They are capable of addressing all standard medical needs the same as a traditional medical doctor; however, they adhere to holistic principles that use a variety of alternative methods to promote physical, emotional, and spiritual health, and encourage a better quality of life." So basically, this is a combination of naturopathic and standard medical practice.

In the United States, naturopathic and most holistic medicine is not covered by insurance and can be expensive. Remember, however, that it is an investment in yourself, in your happiness now and in the future. How you feel physically affects how you feel mentally. It is worth the price.

If you are interested in holistic medicine, here are some resources to find a naturopathic or holistic doctor in your area and some more information about it.

Alternative Medicine
- Books
1. *Alternative Medicine, Second Edition: The Definitive Guide (Alternative Medicine Guides)* by Larry Trivieri, John W. Anderson and Burton Goldberg
2. *Alternative Medicine for Dummies* by James Dillard, Terra Ziporyn
3. *Homeopathic Remedies: A Quick and Easy Guide to Common Disorders and Their Homeopathic Treatments* by Asa Hershoff

- <u>Websites</u>
1. All things holistic:
    http://www.holistichelp.net/holistic-doctors.html
2. Lots of alternative ideas:
    http://www.holistic.com/home
3. Information, how to find a holistic doctor, support:
    http://www.holisticmedicine.org/content.asp?
    pl=2&contentid=2
4. A great site for all things naturopathic:
    http://naturopathic.org/
5. Detailed site about naturopathic medicine:
    http://www.naturodoc.com/cardinal/naturopathy/
    whatisNM.htm

If holistic medicine is not your cup of tea (pun intended), look elsewhere. There are many options and more every day. Research your particular health issues. Consider seeing a nutritionist (which *is* usually covered by insurance). Added to that, consider a trainer if you are out of shape (you can be skinny as a rail and still be out of shape, i.e. me). Another option is a life coach. They focus on your whole life from managing your time and money to getting into shape and nutrition.

Even if you are not interested or unable to see or hire someone, do your homework and do as much of it yourself as you can. An investment in your health is one worth spending, even if all you want to spend is time and energy. Go to the library or your local bookstore and read! Here are some great books and websites I found to get you started.

Easy Get-Started Resources to Get Healthier
- Books
1. *Get Healthy Now! A Complete Guide to Prevention, Treatment and Healthy Living* by Gary Null
2. *How To Lose Weight and Get Healthy Even If You're Lazy – 115 Painless Weight Loss Tips* by Becky Clark
3. *50 Fitness Tips You Wish You Knew: The Best Quick*

and Easy Ways to Increase Motivation, Lose Weight, Get In Shape, and Stay Healthy by Derek Doepker
4. *The Secret* by Rhonda Byrne

- <u>Websites</u>
1. Simple but true advice to be healthier: http://www.wikihow.com/Become-a-Very-Healthy-Person
2. Good article on a lot of simple healthy tips: http://just-healthy.net/
3. A website about the documentary that began my healthy journey (also on Netflix as well as many other documentaries on nutrition): http://www.foodmatters.tv/

Gluten-Free Resources

I figured I would add this section for you gluten-free people like me. According to food.com, gluten is: "The common name of the glutenin protein commonly found in wheat and other cereals made into breads. It is the tough elastic stuff that holds the air created by the yeast."

The more I learn about nutrition and gluten, the more gluten free our whole family has become. For example, did you know wheat in this country has been genetically altered to make it contain more gluten? The reason is it makes puffy breads such as donuts, white sandwich bread, and bagels puff up more. This "super gluten" has become so rampant it has contaminated normal strains of wheat to the point normal strains no longer exist in this country. Some experts believe that is one of the many reasons gluten allergies and celiac disease have become such a widespread problem, or in my case potentially lethal.

Here are some resources on why gluten may be bad for us and how to become gluten free.

- <u>Books</u>
1. *The Gluten Connection: How Gluten Sensitivity May*

Be Sabotaging Your Health – And What You Can Do to Take Control Now by Shari Lieberman
2. *The First Year: Celiac Disease and Living Gluten-Free: An Essential Guide for the Newly Diagnosed* by Jules E. Dowler Shepard
3. *Food 101 – Gluten: What Gluten Is, Why it Affects So Many People, and Natural Ways to Reduce Symptoms of Intolerance* by Kevin Mullani

- <u>Websites</u>
1. A good site for gluten free books and products: http://www.glutenfree.com/
2. All products, information, and support on gluten and celiac diseases: http://www.celiac.com/
3. A good personal blog about living gluten free: http://glutenfreegirl.com/category/are-you-new-to-gluten-free/

Finally, I should note that I do not have Celiac disease. I am allergic to wheat (which contains gluten). Having a gluten or wheat allergy is NOT the same thing as celiac disease. For those like me who are allergic to wheat or gluten or any food allergy, for that matter, another option is to look into allergy drops or antigen drops. These are given as a way to slowly expose you to what you are allergic to so that eventually your body no longer recognizes it as a threat. Similar to an allergy shot, only given by mouth, it is the only legitimate and successful route for food allergies. Google allergy drops to find a facility in your area that carry them. My naturopathic doctor carries them as well.

Stress: What Is It?
- Books
1. *Stress: What It Is, What It Can Do to Your Health, How to Handle It* by Walter McQuade and Ann Aikman
2. *The Cortisol Connection: Why Stress Makes You Fat and Ruins Your Health – And What You Can Do About*

It by Shawn Talbott

3. *The Anxiety Workbook for Teens: Activities to Help You Deal with Anxiety and Worry* by Lisa M. Schab

- Websites
1. Believe it or not there is an American Institute of Stress: http://www.stress.org/what-is-stress/
2. Good site for what stress is in layman's terms: http://www.mamashealth.com/stress/
3. A good website with a lot of information about stress and ways to deal with it: http://lifehacker.com/5836879/what-stress-actually-does-to-you-and-what-you-can-do-about-it

Stress: Ways to Deal with It
- Books
1. *Stress, Anxiety and Insomnia – What the Drug Companies Won't Tell You and Your Doctor Doesn't Know* by Michael T. Murray N.D.
2. *How to Avoid Stress and Live Life to the Fullest: Get To Know What Is Stress, Symptoms And Signs of Stress and How to Manage Stress* by Laura J. Warren
3. *The Relaxation and Stress Reduction Workbook for Kids: Help for Children to Cope with Stress, Anxiety, and Transitions* by Lawrence E. Shapiro Ph.d. , Robin K. Sprague, Matthew McKay

-Websites
1. A good site for simple ways to help with stress: http://www.helpguide.org/mental/stress_management_relief_coping.htm
2. A great site for all things stress: http://www.controlmystress.com/ways-to-deal-with-stress.html
3. A website for kids and teens about how to deal with

stress:
http://kidshealth.org/teen/your_mind/emotions/stres
s.html

HSP: Highly Sensitive Person

According to Wikipedia a highly sensitive person is: "a person having the innate trait of high sensory processing sensitivity (or *innate sensitiveness* as Carl Jung originally coined it) who may process sensory data much more deeply and thoroughly due to a biological difference in their nervous systems." Some of the many traits of a HSP are sensitivity, shyness, creativity, and overactive senses highly in tune to our environment and other people's emotions, etc. For a full list and even a quiz to see if you are an HSP check out the sources below.

- Books
1. *The Highly Sensitive Person: How to Thrive When the World Overwhelms You* by Elaine Aron
2. *The Highly Sensitive Person's Workbook* by Elaine Aron
3. *The Highly Sensitive Person's Survival Guide: Essential Skills for Living Well in an Overstimulating World* by Ted Zeff Ph.D.
4. *The Highly Sensitive Child: Helping Our Children Thrive When the World Overwhelms Them* by Elaine N. Aron

- Websites
1. Elaine Aron is the pioneer of the Highly Sensitive Person diagnosis. Her website has lots of information, including a quiz to see if you might be a HSP: http://www.hsperson.com/
2. A website for us HSPs: http://www.highlysensitivepeople.com/
3. A good website to show and help us to grow our good traits as HSPs:

http://highlysensitive.org/

PTSD, Post-Traumatic Stress Disorder
Most likely you have heard of this disorder. It is usually associated with members of the military; however it can affect anyone who has been through a traumatic event. Post-traumatic stress disorder, according to thefreedictionary.com, is "an anxiety disorder associated with serious traumatic events and characterized by such symptoms as survivor guilt, reliving the trauma in dreams, numbness and lack of involvement with reality, or recurrent thoughts and images." I have suffered from PTSD for over thirteen years, eight of which I suffered in silence having no idea I even had it. PTSD is a serious disorder and needs to be handled by a professional, the sooner after the traumatic event the better. Here are some sources to understand and relate to others with PTSD.

-<u>Books</u>
1. *The Post-Traumatic Stress Disorder Sourcebook: A Guide to Healing, Recovery, and Growth* by Glenn Schiraldi
2. *Conquering Post-Traumatic Stress Disorder: The Newest Techniques for Overcoming Symptoms, Regaining Hope, and Getting Your Life Back* by Victoria Lemle Beckner
3. *The Post Traumatic Stress Disorder Relationship: How to Support Your Partner and Keep Your Relationship Healthy* by Diane England

- <u>Websites</u>
1. This website is geared towards veterans, but it has great info and resources about PTSD: http://www.ptsd.va.gov/
2. A good, straightforward site about PTSD and treatment options: http://www.helpguide.org/mental/post_traumatic_s

tress_disorder_symptoms_treatment.htm
3. An online support group for PTSD (requires free signup):
http://www.dailystrength.org/c/Post-Traumatic-Stress-Disorder/support-group

As a side note, my holistic doctor introduced me to a new (atleast new to me) kind of therapy that has helped me immensely with my PTSD, called EMDR or eye movement desensitization and reprocessing.

How Do You Handle Stress?
As I mention many times in this book, we are all individuals. Each of us handles good and bad stress in different ways. Here are some resources to help you learn how you handle stress and some ways different people handle it.

- Websites
1. This is a quiz that tells how well you handle stress:
http://www.betterhealth.vic.gov.au/bhcv2/bhcarticl es.nsf/pages/Quiz_how_well_do_you_manage_stress
2. A short stress quiz geared towards men:
http://www.menshealth.com/cda/quiz.do? channel=health&conitem=89fcaf1648c5e010VgnVC M20000012281eac___
3. Stress quiz geared towards women:
http://www.youbeauty.com/quizzes/stress

Sources to Help You Get Organized .

- Books
1. *7 Habits of Highly Effective People* by Stephen R. Covey
2. *Get Organized: Smart Solutions on How to Declutter and Stay Organized, Including 100 Quick Tips on Getting Your Life Organized* by Sarah Smith

3. *Organizing Your Day: Time Management Techniques that Will Work for You* by Sandra Felton, Marsha Sims

- Websites
1. http://www.organizeyourself.com/?c=org-m-mi2-12-12
2. http://www.getorganizednow.com/
3. http://www.free-time-management-tips.com/get-organized.html

Healthy Ways to Deal with Stress

How to deal with stress is different for every person. So I will share a list of suggestions for you and let you pick which ones work for you. If you don't like any you see, explore, read, and research until you find what works for you.

- Exercise: walk, run, jog, swim, lift weights, etc.
- Yoga
- Read/Write about it
- Talk about it
- Box it out (literally take a boxing class or go to the gym and punch and kick your stress away)
- Canoe/Kayak
- Take a bath
- Take a nap
- Go to a museum (unless that causes you stress)
- Take a day off
- Plan a vacation
- Put a puzzle together
- Play a board game
- Dream (Imagine something positive happening. Got a promotion. Won the lottery. Got an invitation to a fabulous party. Whatever makes you feel good!)
- Get together with someone you enjoy spending time with.
- Laugh! Watch a funny movie. Read a funny book. Spend time with someone who makes you laugh.

- See **Instant Happiness Triggers** below
- Hire a babysitter and take a night out (or a night in!)
- Look forward to something every day. Find something that you can't wait to do every day even if it is before/after work.
- Art: Color, draw, paint, etc. Even if you have no "talent," so what! Do it for fun!
- Garden/Grow something
- Anything that makes you feel good and/or relaxed

Death Preparedness

*Resources to help prepare children before they experience loss

- Books

1. *Lifetimes: The Beautiful Way to Explain Death to Children* Bryan Mellonie
2. *A Place Prepared: Helping Children Understand Death and Heaven* by Earl A. Grollman
3. *Water Bugs and Dragonflies: Explaining Death to Young Children* by Doris Stickney
4. *Heaven's Not a Crying Place: Teaching Your Child about Funerals, Death, and the Life Beyond* by Joey O' Connor
5. *Pet Loss and Children: Establishing a Health Foundation* by Cheri Barton Ross

- Websites

1. http://www.wikihow.com/Talk-to-Your-Children-About-Death

*Resources to help you with your final wishes
- Books
1. *Organizing Your Final Wishes* by Penelope Spry, Morgan Orr
2. *These Are My Final Wishes* by Tamara Dunkel

- Websites
1. A helpful website that summarizes how to prepare for your own death, virtually: http://mashable.com/2008/01/28/prepare-for-your-death-online-20-helpful-tools/
2. This website talks from a professional perspective on good ideas to ensure your final wishes are carried out: http://money.usnews.com/money/blogs/the-best-life/2011/02/25/how-to-ensure-your-last-wishes-are-carried-out

*Resources to help you prepare for death, when someone you know is dying
- Books
1. *Help! Someone I Love is Dying: A Guide through the Turmoil of Death, Grieving, and Survival* by Clydene Locklear
2. *Saying Goodbye to Someone You Love: Your Emotional Journey through End-of-Life and Grief* by Fredda Wasserman, Norinne Dresser

- Websites
1. The Association for Death Education and Counseling has a searchable database of counselors who are trained to work with the dying and bereaved. http://www.adec.org/AM/Template.cfm?Section=Coping_With_Loss_New_&Template=/CM/ContentDisplay.cfm&ContentID=2962

*Cancer
- Books
2. *Dying in Public: Living with Metastatic Breast Cancer* by Sue Hendler
3. *Not the Last Goodbye: On Life, Death, Healing, and Cancer* by David Servan-Schreiber
4. To help a child who knows someone with cancer:

Because ... Someone I Love Has Cancer by American Cancer Society

- Websites
1. Decisions and tips when caring for someone dying of cancer: http://www.mayoclinic.com/health/cancer/CA0004 8
2. Detailed information about each kind of cancer: http://www.cancer.org/cancer/index
3. Medical signs of someone dying and what do to about it: http://www.webmd.com/healthy-aging/tc/care-at-the-end-of-life-the-dying-process

How to Find and Focus on the Good Things

Have you ever had a day when you just woke up on the "wrong side" of the bed? You didn't sleep well, you don't feel like getting out of bed, and then you oversleep and are frantically running around trying to get to work on time. Sure, we all have. It happens. However, one thing I have learned is that moments like these can either ruin your day or you can "switch" your attitude, brush it off, and have a good day. You can literally teach yourself to think into a good day. As you are frantically rushing around, think: "I am going to make it on time and it is going to be a good day." If you're late anyway, think: "I am late, but it is not the end of the world. I am still going to have a good day." Anytime you find yourself thinking negative thoughts, practice at stopping those thoughts and replacing them with good ones. This can be difficult at first, but start by becoming more aware of your thoughts. You will be surprised how often your thoughts go to the negative. Then like a muscle, exercise your ability to stop your negative thinking and replace it with positive thinking. If it is too hard to think of something positive see the next section titled **Happiness Triggers,** which is a good place to start. Another thing that helped me is to pick a "mantra"—something easy to say, easy to remember and that is positive and uplifting. Some examples are, "All good things are coming my way," or "I am happy and healthy." Even if you don't believe it, just thinking it will help shift you from negative to positive. Try it. It can't hurt, right?

Instant Happiness Triggers

An instant happiness trigger is something that you can focus on or think about that instantly makes you feel a positive emotion. I have a lot of them, but my most commonly used ones are of my family. The way my daughter throws her head back when she is laughing really hard; the way my son pulls his feet up when he is snuggling me like he is trying to crawl into my pocket; when I catch my husband looking at me with love in his eyes; my cat purring. These are all things that make me feel good just when I think about them. Everyone has had moments in their lives or moments they experience every day that make them feel happy. Pick one. Here are some suggestions for your own instant happiness trigger:

- A scene from a movie that made you laugh
- A video online that makes you laugh or feel good every time you see it
- A book that you love (this can be full of many different "scenes" that make you feel happy or loving or joyful, etc.)
- A song that makes you feel good or gives you goose bumps
- A place that you find really relaxing: a hot tub, a waterfall, the woods, the top of a mountain, etc.
- An achievement (won an award, got that promotion, finished a race, etc.)
- Richness in all things. Rich in money. Rich in friends. Rich in time. Rich in food. Rich in love. Pick one or pick them all.
- A picture that you just can't stop looking at or remember very vividly that makes you feel good.
- Use your imagination and your memory. Pick anything that makes you smile just by thinking

about it. You got it!

Happy Places

Right along with happiness triggers are happy places. I talk about this earlier in the chapter titled **Get Started**! A happy place is a place real or imagined that you go to feel good and relax. Perhaps it is a place you have been to and loved or it may be a place you have always wanted to go to. If you have never been there, but wish you could, look it up online or in books. Look at pictures and read stories about it. When you hit a low or want a way to relax, use your happy place. Here are some ideas to get you started:

- A beach
- The woods
- A waterfall
- In a boat
- Meadow of flowers
- A park
- Whatever place makes you feel good and/or relaxed

Miscellaneous Resources
- Books
1. A book that changed my spiritual life: *The Shack* by William P. Young
2. A book that changed my life: *The Secret* by Rhonda Byrne
3. My husband's all-time favorite book: *7 Habits of Highly Effective People* by Stephen R. Covey

- Websites
1. A website for twins who have lost their twins: http://www.twinlesstwins.org/
2. My website where you can sign up for my newsletter: www.Breasbooks.com

There is so much information out there to improve your day and improve your life. Never stop searching, never stop reading, and always remember that in each and every moment of your life, there is always something to grab onto: hope.

My one true wish is that no matter where you are in your grief and in your life that you start your healing journey today.

For more information, to sign up for my newsletter, or to see my other books visit my website:

www.Breasbooks.com

Find me on Facebook:

www.Facebook.com/AuthorBreaBehn

https://www.Facebook.com/pages/Death-Sucks-Life-Doesnt-Have-To/138759956298358? sk=timeline

Follow me on Twitter:

www.Twitter.com/Breasbooks

For some videos on my healing journey:

www.Youtube.com/Breasbooks

Purchase other Black Rose Writing titles at www.blackrosewriting.com/books

and use promo code PRINT to receive a 20% discount.

BLACK❦ROSE
writing™

CPSIA information can be obtained
at www.ICGtesting.com
Printed in the USA
FFOW05n1118090215